mr Bean™

Mr Bean's Guide to London

tiger aspect
PRODUCTIONS
an endemol company

Popcorn
ELT
Readers

New Words

busy

The town is very **busy**.

loud

It's very **loud**!

high

It's very **high**!

place

What's your favourite **place**?

sandwich

That's a big **sandwich**!

station

This is the **station**.

shop

This is my favourite **shop**!

'Be careful!'

Be careful!

Where's the popcorn?
Look in your book.
Can you find it?

mr Bean

Mr Bean's Guide to London

Hello, I'm Mr Bean.
I live in London.

car

Teddy

This is the London underground.

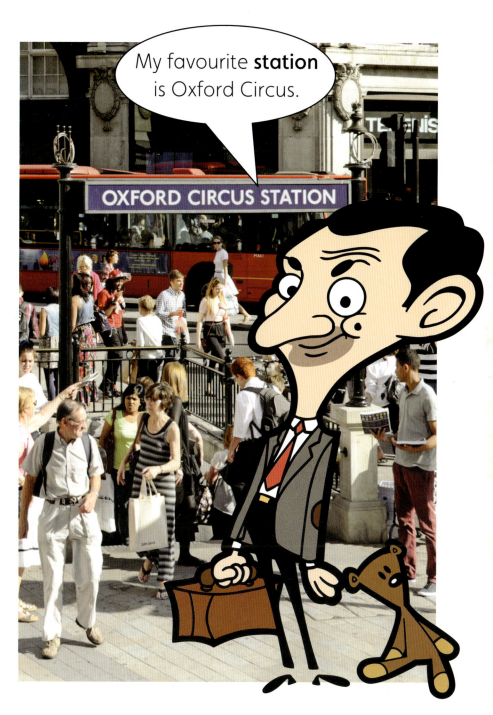

There are a lot of **shops** here.

This is the River Thames.

Look! We can go on a **boat**.

Be careful, Teddy! The water is very cold!

boat

the River Thames

This is the London Eye.

I love the London Eye. It's very **high**!

But Teddy doesn't like it.

Big Ben has a **clock**. What time is it?

It's twelve o'clock.

This is Hyde Park. There are a lot of **pigeons**.

I eat my **sandwiches** here.

Oh no! Stop! That's my **sandwich**!

pigeon

This is Madame Tussauds. There are a lot of **wax models** here.

18

After you read

1 Where is Mr Bean? Match the sentences with the places.

i) Mr Bean has his sandwiches here.

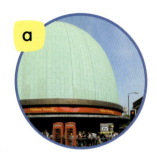

ii) Mr Bean goes on a boat here.

iii) Mr Bean sees William and Kate here.

iv) Mr Bean goes to the shops here.

2 Complete the words. Use the letters in the sandwich.

b

_ a r

c

a

b o a t

_ a t e r

d

_ _ o c k

e

_ _ o p

3a What does Mr Bean say? Write the words.

busy   favourite   high   loud

a) 'It's very busy !'

b) 'It's very .... !'

c) 'It's .... !'   d) 'It's my .... place!'

3b Now draw your favourite place.

My favourite place is ....

Quiz time!

Answer the questions. Yes or No?

		Yes	No
1)	Does Mr Bean like the London Eye?	☐	☐
2)	Does Teddy like the London Eye?	☐	☐
3)	Does Mr Bean have a car?	☐	☐
4)	Does Mr Bean live in Buckingham Palace?	☐	☐
5)	Does the pigeon like Mr Bean's sandwich?	☐	☐

SCORES

How many of your answers are correct?

0–2: Read the book again! Can you answer the questions now?

3–4: Good work! Mr Bean likes you!

5: Wow! Do you live in London too?

Chant

1 🔘 **Listen and read.**

Come to London!

London is big,
London is busy,
Come to London
with me … and Teddy!

Come to the park,
Come to the river,
Come to London
with me … and Teddy!

2 🔘 **Say the chant.**